CROSSROADS

OTHER BOOKS BY DAVID R. SLAVITT

CROSSROADS

POEMS BY

David R. Slavitt

Louisiana State University Press
Baton Rouge and London

1994

03 02 01 00 99 98 97 96 95 94   5 4 3 2 1

Designer: Amanda McDonald Key
Typeface: Garamond & Copperplate 29BC
Typesetter: G&S Typesetters, Inc.
Printer and binder: Thomson-Shore, Inc.

Library of Congress Cataloging-in-Publication Data

Slavitt, David R., date.
    Crossroads : poems / by David R. Slavitt.
        p.   cm.
    ISBN 0-8071-1753-6. — ISBN 0-8071-1754-4 (paper)
    I. Title.
    PS3569.L3C7   1993   93-34589
    811'.54—dc20   CIP

FOR ELEANOR WILNER AND ROBERT WEINBERG

Some of the poems in this volume have been published previously, sometimes in slightly different form, in *Boulevard, Chronicles, Light, Negative Capability, New Criterion, Penn Medicine, Pequod,* and *Prairie Schooner,* and in *Sometime the Cow Kick Your Head* (Bits Press, 1988). "The Penitent Peters" was published in the *Sewanee Review* (CI, No. 1, Winter, 1993). Copyright 1993 by David Slavitt. The author wishes to express his gratitude to the editors of those publications, as well as to the Rockefeller Foundation for a residence at the Villa Serbelloni, where some of the poems were written.

CONTENTS

I

GOING TO GROUND

A green world, buzzing, benign
in hidden glen or hushed glade
where the sun's rays dance on motes
swimming in air like midges, magic,
and, surely, the sound of running water
enlivens the place, an Eden or even
better, our best dream—its serpents
are penises laughing girls have tamed
as amusing pets. There's no such place,
but how can you know when the next rise
could open to show a vista familiar
as childhood's bedroom you still wake to
decades later? (It gives way
to a squalid other, a present you daren't
trust too much.) The arrangements of buildings,
other men's fancies, are arbitrary,
and you deserve and demand more:
a universe that fits you, welcomes,
and celebrates, as your parents did
or ought to have done. If Earth is mother,
however preoccupied and moody,
at least sometimes she must feel for us
something like our tender longing
that calls out for its own completion
and at such relenting moments may
smile and offer us that glimpse
of rocks, trees, hillsides, and sky
disposed to conform and satisfy
our unsuspected expectations.
No mere exercise in landscape,
this vision haunts us all our lives
of how the spirit can inhere,
enlivening the mute and brute
objects we stub our toes on. That green
world is where Viola sorts
Orsino out of all that rumple.
Pamina and her Tamino unite

as we hoped they would—but nothing is ever
certain when all are behaving badly,
Calibans let loose. We all
rely on Rosina's gracious pardon
when she forgives her errant Count
in a song that melts and continues to echo
in us as if a mountainside
itself were singing where we'd choose
to settle—had we not always lived there.

PENTINA: A DRIVE THROUGH A BAD FIVE BLOCKS

Their banal intention is getting drunk or laid,
but who can move in such transfixing heat?
The put-upon set upon each other, then, and fight
or merely threaten to, menace and curse. Morose,
they try to imagine comfort if not fun.

The sun dazzles a gold that washes the lead
of their squalid appointments, as if from a western height
the mercy of heaven itself were seen to have fought
with a stricter justice. But no, it's merely a ruse
and not persuasive here where all's profane

if not obscene. Our parents, we realize, lied
and teachers too. As pavement melts in the hot
truth we are forced to acknowledge, underfoot,
old certainties give way and shimmer. Raise
your eyes, and the very buildings wriggle. Often

we weary of comforts' burden, imagine that load
jettisoned, somehow: in front of some tropical hut,
our poorer but richer selves encounter a fate
utterly other. We respond to the strange duress
enlarged and even ennobled. Desperate and fine,

we could live from moment to moment, dangerous, lewd,
and almost animal lives of love and hate,
impulsive, but weighty in risk of utter defeat.
At a light, we dismiss the idea as mere caprice,
check the doors (locked), and glance at the car phone.

CROSSROADS

for Vera

A lowering sky, a wide expanse of stubble
in empty fields, and two roads crossing where
the village houses, leaning together, huddle
    against cold Polish air:

I see that dour landscape clearly, although
I've never been there. It could be from a story
we tell to children—but then, on second thought, no.
    Why should we have them worry

as we do? Nothing remains of that crossroads
hamlet. One street, I'm told, had the better houses;
the other was where we lived, of course, but those
    gaps close as the time passes.

It was for our sake our grandparents gave it up
and left the place, things, people they belonged to
for the dream of somewhere safer. On the trip
    that thought was what they clung to

for dear life, and, alive, I'm glad they came,
but what they abandoned is what I dream of now,
asleep, while people who don't even know my name
    monitor consoles that show

what zones in my house have been violated—what doors
or windows opened, or motion sensors tripped
by the cat or some intruder. On the street, cars
    are stolen and stripped

by desperate men, wild children. . . . Who can say?
It isn't safe here, or anywhere, and God,
stunned, still mourns at that crossroads, far away,
    where also the dream died

of the Socialists. (The Zionists' went later.)
Over those empty fields, the wind's low moan
keens for those who died there together better
than we die here alone.

IDA

Sweet as apple cider, yes,
but rather dowdy, like a loose housedress
with flowers on it, Ida, she decided,
wasn't her, and she would not abide it.

Many girls reach more or less the same
conclusion and reject the name
their parents happened to give them; only a few
persist in this notion and conjure out of the air
something better. Fred and Adele Astaire
were dancing together then, and they had chic
and style, as much as anyone the week
my mother went job-hunting and had to choose
something to put on the form. Few Brooklyn Jews
were named Adele, but even Brooklyn was
a part of America, with bright promises.
Adele danced into her mind, and it would suit,
she thought, as well as any. Not too cute,
but not too plain, not Ida.
                              Years go by,
she marries, has two children. My sister and I
grow up. At length our father dies, and she
is killed, and only then, when it falls to me
to order her grave marker, do I learn what
her real name was, from her elder sister. But
not real: her friends, her children never knew
Ida was what she once had answered to.
Adele, she chose herself. Therefore, I put
that on the order for workmen to cut
into the stone.
                    And if it is not she?
Then she has eluded the angel, wriggled free,
and is that girl again, out of harm's reach
as when she left Manhattan Beach
that ordinary morning. The subway came,
and on her way to Manhattan, she picked a name.

Whimsical but also brave,
such spirit is not contained within a grave
or troubled by the wearing down
of arbitrary characters on stone.
We are spared too, who have no cause
to blame ourselves for any memory loss
of what we never knew: she remains with us,
inviolate, and nearly anonymous.

LULLABY

The words are worn down to the bare
tune's bones, but the song sounds
in my head in my mother's voice, thin
as if it had carried by some trick
of air over enormous distance.
In the sharp shard remaining, a bird
appears, I assume having flown for miles,
to sit on the singer's foot. It bears
a message, a love letter she thinks.
After a bit of business (the bird
cocks its head, hops, or perhaps
bows) the singer reads the note
the terrible tenor of which we may
have hazarded guesses about already,
given the minor mode of the music.
Her longed-for lover is dead, but the singer
is able to take some solace from
the ridiculous robin or wren (it was not
one of the nasty pigeons my mother
despised). Before departing, the bird
sings a song, and the song stays,
a kind of consolation—absurd,
or so I supposed, but I was a boy
and could not conceive of such a loss
or imagine how people in pain will grasp
in their free fall at anything solid,
some sense impression they can turn to
in trying times of senselessness.
Now I know, and the bird flutters
and sings in my mother's fluty voice
that song I remember her singing her baby
fighting fatigue, reluctant to sleep
and let the world for which he was greedy
go. The bird obeys his script
and takes his perch on the tip of a toe,
lively as ever, The lover is dead,
and the music mourns his loss. The tame

but heartless bird delivers his message
chirping into indifferent air
in which his darker cousins caw
their sterner dirges for which my mother
may have been trying to make me ready,
for the night sky is no nursery
ceiling: its pale and pitiless eye
is not that of a patient parent
watching over her stubborn son
and crooning as he fights against sleep.

DIRGE

for Bunya bat Usher

The silence gapes: we cannot fill it.
Words in the mouth turn to dirt.
Who can imagine what was yet to be said,
or remember what she said, or what we said . . . ?
Not even love can hold it.
       Mute, we are clods.
A mouth agape, a hole forgets itself,
wears down, fills up, as, through a cruel mercy,
it is made whole again.

BOTTOM

Touching bottom, there's nowhere lower to go:
this must be the it we've always dreaded,
and yearned for too, for its certainty. But it
changes, shifts, betraying us yet again
as contours revise themselves; sandbars appear,
erode, and reappear; there are also wrecks.

The harbor's mouth speaks, a mutter of waves
and tides, currents and violent storms that spent
their fury here. Tranquil skies are always
the same, but the sun inspects a new display
of deformities every morning. Turbulence glints
from those surface eddies, and ripples run in the light:
we learn to read and fear them. Each passage out
the tiller throbs as we take our lives in our hands.

THE PENITENT PETERS

for Paul Weiss

1

There are two St. Peters—El Greco's is on the right.
In a dazzle of light, a heavenly scrutiny, he
prays for himself and for all the world, suggested
in schematic boughs overhead, a human figure—
possibly female—off to the left, and way
down the road, a sketchy town, backlit
in the sunset. Lean, aristocratic, gnarled
(look at those arms!) he intercedes for us,
and there the keys to the kingdom hang from his belt.

But across the double doorway of the Phillips
Gallery's music room hangs another Peter,
Goya's, who also prays. And there's no world,
but only a brown background, admittedly paint
of which, he too, is part and parcel. His
is another kind of prayer, and he is another
kind of man, a saint but plump. Low forehead.
A man of the poor people. . . . One could say more.
That he once might have been a Simon, could have been Jewish,
Yiddish, even id-ish. Emblematic keys
are nearby: he has put them down on a rock,
setting aside for a moment a weighty burden.
He prays, I assume, for himself: O Lord, I am not
worthy. But which of us is? And who will take up
on our behalf the heft of those ponderous keys?

2

It wasn't to gain the world that we put our souls
at risk—but only to know that the world is there.
Our body's boundaries bound us, closed us in.
Beyond was mother, was other, and we were othered,
orphaned, as often enraged as enraptured: we sickened
with longing. Goya's Peter, at ease, at home
in his painted world, is already closer to heaven

than anything we can, in bereavement, dream.
He hardly requires those keys he has at hand.

As he prays for the world, he faces the doorway. Across,
in the line of his vision, El Greco's Peter ignores him,
the eyes raised to the source of a blaze of amazing
light. Those representations around him that we
notice, he disregards, having quite taken leave
of all that men have learned to cherish, placate,
and appease—the world's body, which may not be ours,
but reaches toward us as mothers do for children
sick, even to dying. (Aren't we all?)
But he no longer takes notice, has already turned
his eyes away and upward to pray for the world
for us, as he prays for himself, oppressed by the weight
of that light of God in a heaven where there is no
other, and where, at last, we may be healed,
whole, and—though we cannot remember it—home.

CITYSCAPE: WINTER

The snow is a falsification: hard outlines
of objects that glistened in last night's clear cold air
blur, soften, become stuffed toys of themselves.

Their whiteness is also wrong, its purity
specious. Give it a day and dirt will show,
the grey truth of the prosecution's brief

to impeach this testimony. Wan sunshine
prompts bare metal to reassert itself,
and later, when temperatures fall again, your tongue,

if you dared kiss it, would freeze there, stuck forever.

AMPHIBIAN

In tidal pools, the tiniest creatures know
what our children do—how the change from day to night
or dry to wet and the swim in a sea of dream
monsters can terrify. As children are slow
to go to bed, these mussels and barnacles might
complain too, if they could, cajole or scream.

We are skittish at any threshold, to kingdom or room,
which is good reason to teach our children to pray
before they lay them down to sleep and become
meat, or vegetable, matter. No wonder they
are edgy, as we in the mornings are just as unwilling
to move too soon. Like dolphins or great whales breaking,
we loll a while in the light that washes the ceiling,
then hurl ourselves upon the hard beach of waking.

POEMS WRITTEN ON HOTEL STATIONERY

1 LAS BRISAS

A cliff . . . they often put these hotels on cliffs.
Birds dart across the sky making squeaky-toy
cries of delight. (Or are they hungry?) Below,
we see the sea and can descend for lunch
in the shelter of thatch. Outside, in the sun on the sand,
natives trudge, hawk silver bracelets, dresses,
hats, kites . . . One girl sold toy rats.
We repair up the hill where the greatest demand upon us
is the daily death of hibiscus blossoms they put
in the pool each morning to drift and waterlog,
and lack of stress is the only stress. Each day,
we inspect the sunset. Later, we'll have a nightcap
under the stars and over the constellations
of lights below, the town we look down on that clings
to the hem of the mountain's skirts across the bay,
and wonder perhaps what they can dream of down there.
It is up to us to see what those dead eyes
cannot imagine. They take for granted the hot
sand that has burnt their soles to the toughness of shoes.

2 THE INN AT SPANISH BAY

From across the dunes at sunset, a piper skirls:
the simple meeting and merging of fire and water
as the sun drips from the raspberry mille-feuille
confection the sky has become into the silver
foil of the ocean's wrapper is not enough,
so management tries to retain the patrons' attention
by such bizarre grace notes. And the motif is
Scottish, after all. From the golf links: Troon;
St. Andrews; why not a piper? Nevertheless,
the kitchen is northern Italian, some higher-up
having drawn the line, thank God, at haggis. It works,
one must confess, and that nature, naked, requires
tinkering. No place, no event is ever
sufficient unto itself. At Pebble Beach,

tee shirts allude to Maui, as there, to here.
To sit still, to be wholly where we are
and be content even with luxury, sunsets'
spectacular shows of the sky and the sea, demands
too much, is too expensive, exclusive. Heaven!
It's almost all one could want. But it costs the earth.

SUMMER STORM

in memory of R.P.W.

Whatever it was that laid me low last night
with its nausea and headache, I have fought off,
and dawn has broken fair: yesterday's storm
with lightning flashes, thunderclaps, and hail
the size of nickels is barely credible now,
and barn swallows punctuate blue sky.

The great man's night has brought him no such relief.
With stuttering step, holding on to his walker,
he'll be making his way to the toilet, letting slip
those gasps of pain the last sentence or two
of a great work ought not dwindle down to.
The violent storm I weathered, I shall remember
only because it blasted that lofty rotten
tree already leaning into its fall.

MOSQUITO

At the barely audible whine, you pull the sheet
over your head, blitzed, and feel the itch
already on elbow, wrist, or arch. You wave
an ineffectual arm to scare it away
and lie in the dark waiting for it to embolden—
as you know it will—to make its next sortie.
Get out of bed and hunt it? They're fairly stupid,
know only a few tricks, go for height,
and try to hide as benign specks on the ceiling
(a U-boat commander's idea in reverse).
You sweep the theater of operations, woodwork
and moldings they seem to like, approach, slap,
and see the pretty result on your palm, a red
badge. Or bud. What bombardier has not
compared his work to the blossoming of flowers?
But this blood's yours; with it comes satisfaction,
even vindication. These kamikazes
should stay away, on their side of the screen,
out in nature where they belong, but, crazed
and hungry for blood, or looking for easy pickings,
they brave the chinks where the air conditioner housing
isn't flush to the window frame and attack.
Of course, you take this personally and answer
crazy with crazy, even line up their carnage
as trophies on your nightstand. You turn out the light,
sink back, test the silence, and try not to scratch,
not to bloody your wounds, for skin is thin
and doesn't offer much protection from savage
beasts that ever threaten, inside and out.

RAPTURES

To claim the poem as mine would be to tell
only that half-truth that's worse than a lie.
The other, the missing half, which is true as well,
is the poem's claim on me: I know how I

was lured, held for a brief spell in a rapture.
I wasn't myself, but a vessel, a plain tin cup
filled and then suddenly emptied, and cannot recapture
the dazzle of those droplets. I look up

from the poem and can't remember, or only barely,
what it felt like, and what I have lost. What you
approve the most is what afflicts most sorely,
not being me but something I went through

and want not to resent. Enlivened by birds
migrating south, the sky they wheeled upon
is emptier for their passing. These spates of words
leave similar vacancies when they've gone.

ISMENE

Antigone has hanged herself in that dark
cave; Haimon, her fiancé and also
her cousin, is dead too, impaled on his sword;
his mother, Eurydice, also has killed herself;
the entire clan is wiped out except for Creon,
the king, who is also done for, having brought
ruin down on his own stubborn head. He sprawls
on a throne that is after all only a chair
like any other. Nothing is left of the house
and line of Laius . . . except, of course, Ismene,
whom even the dramatist-general Sophocles
has somehow overlooked. Her griefs are greater
than Creon's, but inconvenient: they will not fit
the formula. Pity and terror must keep in proportion,
but nothing's heroic here. She is ordinary;
her *Alltäglichkeit* reaches out and across
the footlights to seats in the amphitheater in which
we perch, believing we're safe from what those others
have been and done, as we could never do,
confronting the cruel Sphinx and finding the right
smart answer? Hardly. And as for the rest,
we worry about it, but only abstractly, knowing
how unlikely it is that we will ever
kill our fathers, marry our mothers, or blind
ourselves to wander the earth as strangers until
the stern gods relent, or that our sons
will slay one another. Those agonies, those actions
are huge, and we are small and give thanks for our small
blessings. But what part has Ismene played
in these grand designs? She suffers, as anyone would,
the griefs of her parents (or should one say her mother
and half brother?) and those of her sister. She's moved
to lie, to try to admit, to share in the guilt
of Antigone's violation of that decree
forbidding to Polynices' body the last
rites—an absurd idea, and it doesn't work.
And she is left, alone, for us to imagine

growing old in Thebes, living on for years
with those three plays in continual repertory
every night in her dreams. Her manic sister's
end is messy, flashier, yes, but quicker.
Depression stretches its pain for her and doles
the day's bearable blows in a formulation
that doesn't kill her, however much she may pray
for that to happen. She speaks her mind in the plays
and tells her father and sister her worst fear:
"You will both leave me behind; I shall have lost
everything, everyone; my heart will break
but beat on; and in utter desolation
 I shall have to make my way, treading on coals."
How can she appear on stage when we have just
passed her out on the street, on our way to the theater,
or today in the market? Some of us know her well
and have learned ways to avoid her baleful face
that every morning stares back at our own.

JOB'S WIFE

My wife's annihilating mind!
—Bink Noll

Consider, in its verso version, Job's
story—as that of his wife, who is never named.
What he suffered, she suffered, but then
she would not be appeased by the new herds
of sheep and camels and all those oxen and asses.
The three new daughters and eventual seven
sons of the whispering concubines, she hated,
mourning her own children, cursing heaven,
and holding fast, as her distracted mate
was unable to do, to the hurt that throbbed
at each beat of her inconsolable heart.
    In the studies and salons
    where we pass our afternoons,
    the fashion is for mannerist
    tales with no vulgar reversals,
    no neat surprises. Truth
    is delicate, its colors pale
    and fading even as we look,
    turning fragile vellum pages
    of life's illuminated book.
But the poetry, the poetry! Surely this
is persuasive, a representation of some
higher wisdom. But is it? When prose gives way
to verse, we should be alert, a little suspicious
whenever reason yields to dramatic gesture.
The famous whirlwind, however impressive, did not
have anything of interest to impart.
It could, of course, intimidate a man,
displaying Behemoth and Leviathan
as examples of its possible excess, odd
but deplorable for how it can disarrange
a life. By such a reversal, Job, undone,
bowed to his pain and made of it a god.
    To women, pain is never a stranger,
    and Job's wife disdained to be dazzled
    by ominous phosphenes that flashed
    as she rubbed her eyes with clenched fists.

Instead, an estranged and difficult
sister, it comes in its good time
to sit in the kitchen in silence or
speak of how new griefs recall
losses nobody knows about.
But she does and remembers them all.
Their lives' preposterous prosperous coda
is not just the conventional folktale's
peripety, but a joke Job never got.
His wife didn't laugh either, although she knew
that faces of children are not like those on cards,
to be shuffled and redealt in a fresh hand.
Men, who can deny anything, will believe
anything—which is surely the point of the story,
the devil's triumph by any sensible reading.
She let him have it, giving her husband over,
having given him up long since as a bad job.

SCORDATURA

Scordatura, literally, "discord," means any unusual
tuning of a stringed instrument.

For the fifteen mysteries Biber's mysterious
scordaturas made the fiddle
sing new resonances, stark
or mellow timbres. It's a trick,
to enable otherwise awkward chords,
make octaves easy, or parallel thirds . . .

The spirit leaps—it always does
at certain kinds of music, at
animal cries, or the wails of babies,
lovers, the newly bereaved. The devil
plays on the fiddles of our heartstrings,
with scordaturas to silence angels
or make them weep. He's showing off
his virtuosity, and we
applaud this instrumentalism
until our red palms sting in the pain
of dungeons, sickrooms, or, on stages,
Oedipus' howls, or Lear's rages.
Their echoes resonate, enlarging
our own distressing repertoires.

THE PRINCE

The prince comes riding in, but we hardly see him.
Nothing in his regular features arrests
attention so much as his horse with its flared nostrils

and billowing mane, conventional representations
of brave action. How can the artist show
intentions and second thoughts as they hang in a balance

more common and exquisite than nobles ever
like to admit? He is not such a stupid fellow
and knows as well as anyone the likely

outcome, should he persist, hacking his way
through brier and vine to arrive at the dark hall
where Sleeping Beauty lies. He will stir up

banked fires his kiss will tongue into flame.
He can't turn back, admits to being a fool
for setting forth, but is disinclined to add

cowardice to his sins. The story unfolds
for him, as it does for us, and he presses on
further into her dream of his arrival

although he is wide awake. He knows what he's doing
as he stands before her, barely hesitates,
then mans himself and reaches forth to rouse her.

TATIANA, OLDER

The innocent passion she has lost hangs on
taking us in, who remember our own and mourn
that such transports are gone. Onegin, remember,
was not even there. That he was clearly queer
was beside the point as she went on and on,
enjoying her suffering even more than we,
for loving is always better than being loved,
however the plot comes out.
                                        The soprano alive
at the end of the last act? Qu'est-ce que c'est?
The young suppose it is sad, that their timing is off;
we know better, as Tatiana also
by this point understands. At the end, her charm
is that she has married the prince, is rich beyond reach,
so he may echo her songs of desire and pass
to the world, and himself, as straight.
                                        It is entertaining
to be adored and to spurn—for his own good—
his absurd advances. Revenge may have some note
in the complicated score, but we may imagine
Tatiana at least toys for a time with the notion
of miracles and conversion: all he needs
is the love of a good—and sufficiently attractive—
woman! But no, that's nonsense, as she knows,
from that Liebestod of a duel. It was never her sister,
Olga, but Lenski, himself, with whom Onegin
flirted that night.
                                        And now it is mostly tact,
or is she in this last scene, sentimental,
imagining how it might have been otherwise?
We do not have to choose: Tchaikovsky allows us
to come as close as we care to (or we dare to).
Laughter, suppressed and bitter enough, can hurt
as much as any of tragedy's bloody conclusions.
But Pushkin had it right: one can hear, offstage,
the jingle of the prince's spurs on the stairs
as he returns, lordly, boring, and real.

BIG BIRD

The osprey (or sea eagle, or ossifrage—
it means bonebreaker) mates, it has been reported
by astonished observers, two hundred times a day.
This mechanism is thought to have been developed
by males in order to occupy, as it were,
their osprey mates. Bastard birds are rare,
but it takes a good deal of effort—every 7.2
minutes. Allowing for naps, the intervals
are probably shorter. When I was a younger man,
I thought of sex nearly that often, but now
feel for the poor bonebreaker, barely able
to hunt, or eat, his entire life so focused,
a degree of regret (and, for myself, relief).
Still, at random moments, more rarely than every
seventh minute, a shadow will flit across
the sky of my mental landscape or seascape,
as from the powerful stroke of a large seabird's
wing, as he hones, homes in, his eagle eye
fixed on that singular truth he perseverates,
signing the sky, of himself and his keen kind.

GREETING TO A GRANDDAUGHTER

What is a man to make of a daughter's daughter?
Infant now, but when her words do come
they will flow like blood, like milk, and mean something else
from what I mean or my sons, or my son's son.
Grace, yes, but with strangeness her mother taught her . . .
or was she born with it, like those ova, cells

already in place and ripening to a future
longer than mine? My mother is gone; I do not
hear from my sister these days; your grandmother and
I are a dismal story that would not suit
your little ears. Your mother can give you what
you yowl for, eyes closed tight. I understand
such helplessness and, speechless, weep and bless
the foreign heart that races in your chest.

SENTENCE

The bread was stale, her father explained—no good.
Sixteen months old, she considered this,
processed the information, and then announced,
"Eat bread, duck-ducks," referring to mallards
that scrounge on the pond in the college garden they visit,
my daughter, son-in-law, and she, my daughter's
daughter. A rather Latinate trick, to hold
in suspense her emphatic subject, but she will learn
handier ways to modulate and stress.
Still, her meaning was clear and clearly beyond
the first business of pointing, of sticking labels
to objects: baba (bottle); bow-bow (dog);
or baby. Better and better articulating,
clarifying like cloudy tap water that stands,
there were nouns first and, later, modifiers:
"Elena's book," or simply a "blue hat."
But this is something new and utterly other,
with subject, verb, and object dancing now
behind her glittering eyes. It is not the wrath
of Achilles, or man's first disobedience and
the fruit of that forbidden tree, not yet,
but it's what she needs in order for them to happen.
Call it the plain the citadel looks out on,
or the empty sea beyond at which they stared,
shielding their eyes for their first glimpse of a mighty
armada rumor had said was on its way.

MUSEUM OF SCIENCE: DISCOVERY ROOM

for Hannah and Isaac

The hamsters burrow into their newsprint or hide
in the cardboard tubes for paper towels, but the huge
gerbil has nowhere to flee to, no refuge
except a useless and desperate one—to decide

to see with his beady eyes the truth reversed
and let the children be exhibitions for him,
a demonstration parading past for his dim
delight. In such earnestness are we all immersed,

afloat for a time, but then awash and drowning,
that we wait for the room to empty out each day,
those monsters of self-improvement to go away
and darkness to come to soothe our anxious frowning.

CAPE COD SNAPSHOT

1

On dunes I've walked, a small girl picks her way
through clumps of beach grass, giving no special thought
to winds that send her red hair streaming, for wildness
is everywhere. She knows she must watch her step.

The way the picture is organized, with the small
white dress in the center of green grass
and dun sand and red hair against the deep
blue of beach sky, is arresting. She

is beautiful. That she happens also to be
my granddaughter is almost beside the point,
which is that the space is all but overwhelming;
that the wind, indifferently tousling hair and grass,

is dangerous; that we must snatch from its powerful
jaws whatever we can. Our eyes are down,
like hers, to find a path, but we look up
at such moments as this. The photograph

enlarges, one might say who didn't claim
kinship, as I do. But I wasn't there, could not
have pressed a button to freeze or seize this image
from the slipstream of her hurtle through childhood.

That intent look on her face comes to me finished,
as if I were a stranger. I must deconstruct,
reconstruct, and claim it. I stare at it hard
with swimming eyes, and try to enter the picture,

to pick my way with her among the hazards
of height, of sea's and sky's vertiginous space,
as winds blow our hair and billow our skirts'
composure. . . . How can one breathe in all that air?

2

She's long gone, that smallness shrunk to a speck,
floating, drifting out of the field of vision.

That sand has been smoothed to glittering blankness except
for this photograph, which helps to even the score

I keep in my head, a running tally of wrongs
like waves that break on the beach below her feet,
not without effect as they eat it away,
cut new channels, erode the Cape, erase it

as I should like to do. I reach for a pen
to work once more the trick of a giant squid
with tentacles and black ink—reach out, clutch
to my greedy head another delicious morsel

the current has offered or others have let slip.
This last word, always mine, may be a hollow
triumph, distorted, even a joke at my own
expense, but if a child takes up a pencil

and plays the vandal, drawing in a mustache
and big glasses, he signs the image, turns it
around, undoes stern faces that loom, and tames them,
as well as he can, to the harmlessness of toys.

II

TO HIS BOOKS

His books desert him, running off like children
to play, to live, languish or thrive, but leaving
their parent home alone to wonder why
he ever cared. Their stylized jacket photos
seem less and less familiar or, what's worse,
are someone else's trophies.

Unpleasant to admit it, but padding along
the harem halls in pursuit of his fancy, he never
gave thought to the issue of those encounters. Let them
fend for themselves then; if they send small checks
from time to time, good manners will prevent him
from expressing great surprise.

AUTHORITY

When I hear the word "culture," I reach for my revolver.
—H. Goering

These fine discriminations are finally vexing;
the blather about this nuance or that,
this reading or that or, let's be frank, my reading
or others' (yours for example) erodes the spirit,
wears one's patience away.

                    Toward the end of his life,
Rodzinski carried onto the podium always
a gun in his pocket, a small-caliber pistol,
not to be used or even brandished to threaten
the players, but felt, its heft there on the hip,
the pleasing sag of his trousers slightly askew
a reassurance, a comfort. The cellos rasped?
The maestro could smile, imagine himself producing
his baton's enforcer, and then the bang, the cry,
the blood, and at last, from survivors, assent, and the heavens'
music he heard in his head and had to struggle
to get from these overpaid, temperamental sons
of bitches, the bastards one has to make do with
for beauty's sake and art's.

JEUX D'ESPRIT

1 MUSEUM CLERIHEWS

Ingres
never painted with his fingres

or van Gogh
with his togh,

although Sisley
did so quite easily

(and Gauguin?
Hein!).

2 INTERMISSION GREETINGS AT THE PARIS OPERA, 1898

"Allo!"
said de Falla to Lalo.

"Hi ya,"
Ed replied to de Falla.

"You're looking quite well,"
each remarked to Ravel,

who, that very day,
had greeted Fauré.

3 TRANSATLANTIC FLIGHT

When it is now there, it will be then here,
but it is not now there yet.
Later it will be now there;
then it will be then there.
But then it will not be then here,
and then it will not be then there
or anywhere, ever again.

THREE IMITATIONS FROM CATULLUS

XLII To an Editor

O skill, o naughty tongue, I need you now
to help me get my words, my work back.
That woman has kept my manuscript for months,
claims she can't find it.
         How can I shame her
so that she'll hand it over? Stand at the door
of her office building and shout at her every morning,
every lunchtime, coming and going, and then
every evening: "Bitch! Whore! Slut!"?

She smiles, waves, is flattered by my attentions.

I hand out cards with her name and "Erotic Massage"
(her direct-dial number is down at the bottom).
She just gobbles it up. What can I do?

At my wits' end, I try changing my tack
with "Maiden," "Gracious Lady," and such old-fashioned
compliments as I can devise.
         She hates it,
wouldn't want her sisters in NOW to know
she puts up with such drivel. I get my poems
back, hand delivered, in less than an hour.

LVII The Midnight Oil

A perfect pair, those two!
         Each deserves
the other: their crabs, I fancy, mingle and mate
when, after hours on that filthy office sofa
incapable of further stain, they exchange
dreadful poems, juicy bits of department
gossip, and assorted bodily juices.

A perfect pair!

Never to promise anything—that's chaste
   and admirable;
or to promise and then deliver—that's handsome
   and therefore, in its way, admirable.
But you Aufilena?
You promise, take, and then never come across.
It's the oldest con in the world you're running there.
Any honest hooker would call it nasty.

NOVELISTS AND POETS

Novelists sign contracts, settle in
to marriage and its routines. Or, happy sappers,
their habit is to besiege, to delve their way
to certain glory. Of course, they distrust poets,

surface creatures, lounge lizards who wait
for the right suggestion to introduce itself,
half-realized, and not excessively forward.
Dreaming with one eye open, they sleep around.

Each looks askance at the other and longs
to be carried away like that. Or to stay put.
A few, who combine the two careers, have twinges
of bad faith either way, and a good time.

THE GIG

On a tippy table, here at the Penn State Days
Inn, I've been scribbling, mostly to pass the time. . . .
It's hardly what those would-be M.F.A.s
imagine, or want to do, who think that I'm

curmudgeonly, or frivolous, or tired,
and resent being discouraged. And what if they do
get published and, on the strength of that, are hired
to teach creative writing (and one or two

sections of bonehead English)? Will I owe
apologies? Or will they also come
to such a pass and room as this and know
envy, resentment, and, worst of all, the numb

indifference that conspires with our own distaste
for readings in ugly lecture halls to sad
small groups, like all the others that we've faced,
impassive, if not sullen, ill read, ill clad,

as their instructors are, who never smile
or even get the jokes but talk of deals,
and publishers, and resent displays of style?
Why condescend to do it, then, if it feels

so bad, and worse all the time? One owes it to
the work? Of course not! But necessity
sneaks up from behind to bite you: you come through
to help a son with dentist's bills that he

can't manage. Therefore, I contrive a grin
with my own expensive teeth. I'll do my show-
and-tell and then get through the party in
my honor. Checking again the impossibly slow

minute hand of my watch, I'll long to get back
to this Days Inn and to quiet—my natural

habitat. Both flattery and attack
I shall endure with an abstract rictus and all

the grace I can muster, keeping my mouth shut,
for there's nothing to say, so long as they're hoping for
tricks of the trade—there are no tricks, and it's not
a trade. Imagine silence. A page turns. More

silence again. That's it. That's all there is.
And yet, from beyond the lamp's charmed circle, faces
are peering, the garish light of the lit biz
having lured them from their usual hiding places.

They're hungry for my secrets? Unearned income
is the most important; then, to have griefs like mine
for which there is no cure, though there can be some
respite with pen and paper's anodyne.

That's not what they want, is surely too much to handle,
but all I have, a gift not of my choosing,
and if no one seems to think it worth the candle
to learn to write well just to be amusing,

there's no help for them, or hope for their poems and
stories, those recitations, thinly disguised,
or betrayals they've suffered from parent or boyfriend
behaving badly. I was not surprised

by any trope or image of theirs. Then why
do they persist? What is the use? They are sad
poster children for some disease you and I
have never heard of. They have got it bad,

but I do, too, I suppose, am a chronic case,
no longer contagious, but that is what confuses
or even annoys. Too bad, but I'll leave this place
with a check for my son—worth a few new bruises.

AN EXTREMELY SHORT HISTORY OF CHINA

for Sophie Wilkins and Karl Shapiro

T'ANG DYNASTY

Suffering, suffering, squalor, suffering, flood, suffering, suffering, really severe suffering, war, suffering, suffering, drought, famine, suffering, brutal suffering, really terrible suffering, a slight diminution of suffering, a few years of reasonable life, the birth of some hope, the revival of the arts and crafts, and then corruption, disaster, war, and flood, drought, and more suffering.

FIVE DYNASTIES ERA

Suffering, suffering, squalor, suffering, flood, suffering, suffering, really severe suffering, war, suffering, suffering, drought, famine, suffering, brutal suffering, really terrible suffering, a slight diminution of suffering, a few years of reasonable life, the birth of some hope, the revival of the arts and crafts, and then corruption, disaster, war, and flood, drought, and more suffering.

SUNG DYNASTY

Suffering, suffering, squalor, suffering, flood, suffering, suffering, really severe suffering, war, suffering, suffering, drought, famine, suffering, brutal suffering, really terrible suffering, a slight diminution of suffering, a few years of reasonable life, the birth of some hope, the revival of the arts and crafts, and then corruption, disaster, war, and flood, drought, and more suffering.

YÜAN DYNASTY

Suffering, suffering, squalor, suffering, flood, suffering, suffering, really severe suffering, war, suffering, suffering, drought, famine, suffering, brutal suffering, really terrible suffering, a slight diminution of suffering, a few years of reasonable life, the birth of some hope, the revival of the arts and crafts, and then corruption, disaster, war, and flood, drought, and more suffering.

MING DYNASTY

Suffering, suffering, squalor, suffering, flood, suffering, suffering, really severe suffering, war, suffering, suffering, drought, famine, suffering, brutal suffering, really terrible suffering, a slight diminution of suffering, a few years of reasonable life, the birth of some hope, the revival of the arts and crafts, and then corruption, disaster, war, and flood, drought, and more suffering.

CH'ING DYNASTY

Suffering, suffering, squalor, suffering, flood, suffering, suffering, really severe suffering, war, suffering, suffering, drought, famine, suffering, brutal suffering, really terrible suffering, a slight diminution of suffering, a few years of reasonable life, the birth of some hope, the revival of the arts and crafts, and then corruption, disaster, war, and flood, drought, and more suffering.

REPUBLIC OF CHINA

Suffering, suffering, squalor, suffering, flood, suffering, suffering, really severe suffering, war, suffering, suffering, drought, famine, suffering, brutal suffering, really terrible suffering, a slight diminution of suffering, a few years of reasonable life, the birth of some hope, the revival of the arts and crafts, and then corruption, disaster, war, and flood, drought, and more suffering.

PEOPLE'S REPUBLIC OF CHINA

Suffering, suffering, squalor, suffering, flood, suffering, suffering, really severe suffering, war, suffering, suffering, drought, famine, suffering, brutal suffering, really terrible suffering, a slight diminution of suffering, a few years of reasonable life, the birth of some hope, the revival of the arts and crafts, and then corruption, disaster, war, and flood, drought, and more suffering.

GALLOWS HUMOR

Depend upon it, sir, when a man knows he is to be hanged in a fortnight, it
concentrates his mind wonderfully.

—Dr. Johnson

To concentrate the mind and gather one's scattered wits,
    there is always Dr. Johnson's prescription: the gallows or any of its
contemporary versions—the clatter of jackboots at night
    that may or may not stop outside your door, or the pause of the white-
labcoated surgeon to consult his book as he picks you a date
    that looms larger as it approaches, and deeper, a chasm, a great
abyss you cannot imagine getting across, though you try
    to be brave and behave like a grown-up. (Odds are you are not going to
die.)
But, as long as you've got to do this, you wonder whether the prospect,
    in a fortnight's time, of the rope or knife will have its predicted effect,
and are disappointed. You worry that it's your fault that there's no
    intellectual laser beam that can cut through murk to show
you what you never knew you knew. The concentration is rather
    poorer, as you are wholly engrossed in your body's inner weather,
and attend to the sound of breathing and jog-trot rhythms of heart
    pumping the blood around to all those organs that, if they were smart,
would rebel, recruiting the legs to run, or the mouth to speak
    the No that is, of that concentration's wisdom, your unique
trophy. You can't read, can barely understand what's said
    on sitcoms on the rental TV that hangs above your head;
and the *Times* is reduced to its crossword; you fidget and deal a new
    hand of Klondike, as if to kill the time that is killing you.
Imagination, caught in necessity's web, may try
    to wriggle free or simply, by brute force, sunder the tie
that tethers us all. . . . Or another and older metaphor
    proposes itself, a filament and an old crone wielding her
glittering shears to trim lifelines, and in with fear
    resentment mixes and envy of those who are healthy and, when they hear
the PA speaker's announcement that visiting hours are done,
    can say good-bye to the patients and, outside, frolic, laugh, run,
and rejoice in their own good fortune, relieved that this is not
    their time of trial, But even this rather meanspirited thought
gutters and dies away as you turn your attention to
    the nerves' reports of pain or distention in what is no longer you
or even yours but just a body someone assigned
    at random, a temporary housing unit in which your mind

is quartered, to which it has been condemned, and there's no appeal.
   But not even that conceit persists very long, for now you feel
worse, do nothing but feel, are a mere sensorium
   in a midway of macabre experience, vulgar, deplorable, dumb,
but that's what life has turned out to be, and you discover
   that your body shares your impatience, is as eager as you for this to be over,
one way or another. That concentration that Johnson
   remarked on, you have reached, but it's not so great a revelation.
One's wit, or more nearly correctly, one's spirit arrives at last
   at its own crucial decision: should it persist in holding fast
to this imperfect baggage or have done and let go
   as a flame will when its candle's tallow is spent? Is it Yes or No?
Stupid greed on the one hand, and maybe habit, fight
   with fatigue on the other, and there is by no means a wrong answer or right,
but you decide, perhaps by flipping a coin, and that one
   moment of focus enlarges like a beam of light that has been thrown
through lenses and prisms upon a wall. Your life returns in its rich
   palette of colors and range of textures, that paraphernalia which
hardly seemed important to you, but now you rejoice
   in having it all restored as if, having made your simple choice,
you had somehow earned the world, but you know that isn't true,
   for what you learned was that nothing out there has much to do with you.

CANZONE

Letters wheel like birds, then settle to spell
words, from which remarkable primary feat
others follow, for words can make a spell
to entrance the world, enchant it, and by their spell
turn it tame, obedient, by grace or
luck, transformed, if but for a brief spell,
coaxed by our blandishments and roused to its pel-
lucid and perfected state. Wounds heal
at the wizard's muttered incantation and he'll
maybe wave his wand, although the spell
doesn't need it, for words will leap from the leaves
of the volume in his hands, and, if he believes,

make the walls of his cell quiver like leaves
in the wind outside his window, by his spell
as alive as the tree. There's nothing up his sleeves.
Language, naked, roused from its slumber, leaves
the cave of its making to manage again that feat
for which it is known—but which of us believes
those fairy tales anymore? We may watch the leaves
of the book on the nightstand twitch in coincidence, or
is there a draft? Deep in the mind's mine, ore
from hidden veins still gleams. A parent leaves,
turns out the light, and close upon her heel,
a spirit appears to dance in the dark, to heal

the day's abrasions, or maybe to punish. (He'll
terrify either way.) What child believes
in mercy, or doubts he's worthless and a heel,
deserving of punishment? The room will heel
crazily, like some fun-house chamber. A spell
or prayer may right it, if said right, may heal
even that fated wound one's Achilles heel
invites and perhaps deserves. It is a feat
we may have dreamt—a dance that the world's feet
never forget. And it still comes to heel

at the word it recognizes, whispered or
prayed in perfect silence. Think of an oar

dipping silent into thought's lake. Or
better, think of how sailboats may heel
in wind too faint to feel. But there's an or-
molu shimmer astern, the sunset's ore
of the kind Rhinemaidens yield when the tenor leaves
the stage to silence. Or sometimes they'll restore
those toys we thought long lost, and still mourned for,
for darkness has gifts too. Recite the spell
and wait and watch for the monsters' rout, as pell-
mell they flee, not quite destroyed but hors
de combat for the moment. Their defeat
encourages you. Crack open a Lafite-

Rothschild, or maybe a Margaux, for that feat
deserves a toast, a feast. But arrogance or
smugness carries the seeds of your defeat:
the charm is not reliable. An effete
practitioner will talk of technique; he'll
criticize vowel values and count feet,
as if that pattern of Arthur Murray feet
on the floor were the dance itself—but the spirit leaves
abruptly, and the world no more believes
in magic, will not be swept off its feet
by incantations. You can't cast your spell
ever again, have fallen under a spell

yourself that you are powerless to dispel.
Your flights are ended. Now, with heavy feet
you trudge the dusty roads, despairing, or
what's worse, clinging to hopes that you may heal
like Tasso's blasted oak and sprout new leaves.

KILLING TIME

With fragile coils, they venture to snare not merely
Love or Thursday afternoon or the sudden
glints of light on wind-ruffled water, but it,
the monster itself, that ravages, terrorizes . . .
Heavier weapons are useless; to go bare-handed
is certain death; therefore these desperate measures
are not altogether mad. And they do come back—
when they come back—with small game, and we drink
and feast for days as if the beast were dead.
There are losses of course, wounds, even deaths. Of these
nobody speaks. What would there be to say?

2

To learn the refinements of new loops and new knots,
we study the work of masters and practice, practice,
but our fear they still feel. Their eyes are hard
to read but hardly serene as they gaze into
thickets where some rustle may or may not
be only the wind. Not to learn their skills
may make sense, but one must be brave to admit
sheer helplessness, one's fate as the clock ticks
little nicks and gashes, sunsets drip
blood, and each new moon is born in blood.

We cannot stop but may put off the monster
by its own caprices: utterly worthless glitter
can turn it from its path. It hesitates,
prods, pummels, and plays, or seems to, while we
stand breathless, trying to gather the courage
to risk a half step backward. Every second
counts. (What else is a life?) And then the bauble
breaks, or it bores him; he lets it roll away;
bloodlust returns to his almost intelligent eyes
fixed on throats in which our screams are frozen.

4

From the yarns we swap, a pattern perhaps emerges
of what it prefers, or what it has liked lately—
as if it were consistent, as if tomorrow
the same tricks might work. The surest bet
is rage, or the fearlessness of having suffered
losses already, so that one's own life is of no
account. Indifference—it cannot be feigned—works:
the beast is able to smell it, isn't afraid,
but shows it a certain respect, lumbering by
as if it were unaware of you standing there.

5

Desperate, we turn to one another, bargain,
promise to save one another, but know we'll betray
and be betrayed. Nothing will keep us alive
but prayers on our children's breath and their guttering candles—
and these are provisions anyone makes! The craft,
those dangers we've shared together have brought us no
special dispensation. Your more or less friendly
faces blur together and start to resemble
that other face, feral and mean, we thought
we were hunting as it was hunting us.

6

No, that's wrong. The beast makes its forays,
but the damage I do myself costs more, hurts more.
Reckless of tomorrow, tomorrows, as if
there were no end of tomorrows, I have let go
a grasp that should have been tight as a drowning man's
on a dory's line. My hands clench upon nothing.
The pictures are faded, the negatives gone like breath
on a cold pane that frosts and then clears. How
can we hold anything dear fast except
by these twists, hitches, crude hooks, and jottings?

7

Not only names and dates but entire scenes,
rooms, meals, clothing, even the beds,
those intimate details biographers love,
are shy, but to pathological lengths. They are self-
effacing, self-destructive. Like suicidal

lemmings, they leap from cliffs to disappear
in an ocean of undifferentiation. Thieves!
Assassins! It is my life they have destroyed.
What can you do with a brain infested with weevils?
Torn between greed and disgust, save what you can.

8

It's not just me. It's these times: who is not
depressed is stupid. Writing's a business, hobby,
tic, or therapy not otherwise worth
the bother. Books on the shelves disintegrate, acid
paper eating itself. No Virgil presides,
ready to guide the way through our dark wood,
and which of us would believe it if he showed up
this afternoon in a toga looking like James
Mason or Claude Rains, to say what we do
isn't, as we'd supposed, merely "inutile"?

9

Virgil is said to have built a series of wooden
statues, one for each province, each of them holding
a bell to ring to warn of trouble at home.
On the roof a brazen horseman brandished a spear
it could point toward any danger. They called these wonders
Rome's salvation. His garden walls were immobile
air—the same exotic substance he'd fashioned
bridges of to take him wherever he wished.
To read with such dumb faith, to pore over texts
in the hope of salvation, to be a child again,

1 0

who wouldn't trade sophistication for that?
For the dear past redeemed, the dread future
forestalled, and the present gentled, we'd take the risks
of Virgil's impossible bridge. I admit to rare
occasions when sunshine dazzled diamonds in morning
air on a spider's not so fragile web,
the engineering of that ascent. But doubt
is our only passion now: as the sun climbs higher,
those cables disappear, and nothing can hold
even an ordinary moment's splendor.

SCREAM

—non lingua valet, non corpore notae
sufficiunt vires nec vox aut verba sequuntur:
—*Aeneid* 12.911–12

1

Horrible dreams—have there been three now? Or four?
Enough for a lifetime, their exquisite terror, more
than mind can bear: I turn, struggle, and writhe
as the monstrous details dive back to their lair,
deformed and deforming—having first extorted
my racked groans. I was attempting screams
but forced the air through a useless larynx, frozen
nearly to muteness. Still inside the dream,
all I could make was the high hoarse noise of a stricken
beast. My wife awoke and came to my aid.

2

That noise I produced was the basis of all speech,
an inarticulate cry that is vessel for each
elaboration and nuance we all value
(perhaps too highly). Who cares, when the object
is the sound itself? To voice the terror loudly
enough may force someone off, or scare him away,
or call for someone's help. The earth was silent
until some primitive creature first rasped hairy
legs together, or chirred, or gasped with . . . what?
Love and joy? Fear, more like, or anger.

3

Grammar, later, separated my fear
from yours and gave directions to the ear,
as if we were not all threatened together.
Bad things happen. Do you run? Or fight?
A groan ruptures the primitive phlegmy silence
each time that question arises, or snarl or whine,
and intricate whorls of the ear and folds of the brain
sort out the situation. Such interjections
don't conjugate or decline, are children of silence
that looms behind them, just out of sight and hearing.

4

But we are all children of screams: our mothers pierced
the air with complaint in labor, to which our first
thin wails added descants. The cries we heard
at birth we carry with us, a burden worth
its weight in gold. Their truth is the touchstone
for all subsequent noise. I have heard my children's
moans in the night. . . . From fears that troubled their dreams,
I could not protect them: I could not protect my mother
and cannot defend myself. That initial scream's
open parenthesis closes at last with another.

5

As children we could endure what we barely knew,
although now we deny we ever gave thought to
such nonsense as the terror of being buried
alive—a long-odds risk, after all. But the fear
is real: of silence, of not being able to voice
our rage in God's name, or rather in God's face.
Drowning is also nastily silent, for one
wants resonance, to shriek an instant in air.
It's little to ask, when all other hope is gone.
Defiance, at that pitch, is a kind of prayer.

WELLIVER'S TREES

Those trees, those rocks are flesh—as he made clear
in earlier paintings in which, from a pool's lush blue,
a woman emerges, her body the world's body,
her hills, thickets, and clefts, the Allagash
he taught us thus to love. Then the woman is gone,
and we are required by his sheer force of will
to make the connections—rock, to flesh, to spirit,
each one painting the next—for the mind is restless,
and, as the delighted eye lights, settles, and revels,
the image will shimmer with truths we can barely bear.

These fire-swept trees' brutal verticals slash
downward, bars on the window through which, condemned
to suffer, we see, in the distance, the green of a hill
we shall never reach. Nature, of course, will recover,
but how can a painting change? This heat, this cold
accuse our temperate habits. Plunge a hand
into that water of Black Brook, or the Head
of Passagassawaukeg. It will turn numb
as the wood, as the rock you need to be to endure
the buffets of weather and time in these deep woods.